Arctic Ocean
Colville River
Noatak River
Kobuk River
Koyukuk River
Yukon River
Fairbanks
Yukon River
Tanana River
Mt. McKinley
Susitna River
Kuskokwim River
Copper River
Anchorage
Nushagak River
Skagway
Gulf of Alaska
Juneau
Bristol Bay
Kodiak Island
Pacific Ocean
AF531092

Klondike Gold Rush National Historical Park

By

By Julie Johnson and Nora L. Deans

Alaska Geographic Association
Anchorage, Alaska

Alaska Geographic Association thanks Klondike Gold Rush National Historical Park for their assistance in developing and reviewing this publication. Alaska Geographic works in partnership with the National Park Service to further public education and appreciation for national parks in Alaska. The publication of books, among other activities, supports and complements the National Park Service mission.

Authors: Julie Johnson, Nora L. Deans
Illustrations/Maps: Denise Ekstrand
Image Credits: Alaska State Library: 11: Winter and Pond Photograph Collection, ASL-P87-0661; 20: PCA 232-80; 40: Eric Hegg, P41-175; 49: Historical Collections, ASL-P277-001-009; 57: Skinner Foundation Photograph Collection, P44-6-222. © John Conforth: 16-17. 2010 © Fred Hirschmann: ii, iii, 50-51, 53, 54, 60, 62-63. © John Hyde: 14, 17 inset lower right. © Nick Jans: 17 inset upper right. 2010 © Mark Kelley/AlaskaStock.com: 8. © Robert Lowe: 17 inset lower left. 2007 © Clark James Mishler/AlaskaStock.com: 44. Library and Archives Canada: cover, C-004489; 6, Edward Bros. (?)/ C-016460. Library of Congress: 39, LC-USZ62-30616. Museum of History and Industry, All rights reserved: 31: 88.33.116; 35, upper: SHS1688; 61: 1986.5.1208.1. National Park Service: 1: (newspaper); 13: (map), 26 upper, 52, 58 all, 59. © RonNiebrugge/www.wildnatureimages.com: 7,15. Skagway Museum: 27: PC 93.02.237. University of Alaska Fairbanks, Rasmuson Library, Archives, Alaska and Polar Regions Collections: 23: UAF-76-133. University of Washington Libraries, Special Collections: 2: UW8410; 3: Hegg 553; 6 Hegg 156; 10: A. Curtis 46161; 12: Klondike 214; 25: Hegg 314B; 33: A. Curtis 345A; 34: A. Curtis 11093-1; 35 lower: UW5801; 36: Hegg 207; 37: Hegg 96; 38: Hegg 3101; 41: UW563; 42: Hegg B576; 43: Hegg 20A; 45: Hegg 540; 46: CUR2001; 47: A. Curtis 46118; 48: Hegg 17A; 55 lower: UW11702; 56: UW14796. Washington State Historical Society: iv-1: 46036, 28-29: 46053. Candy Waugaman, Fairbanks, Alaska: 18-19, 30, 32 (photo by Debbie Whitecar). Yukon Archives: 4-5: Anton Vogee fonds, 109; 9: Eric Hegg fonds, 2667; 24: Anton Vogee fonds, 103; 48 lower: H.C. Barley fonds, 4906; 55 upper: H.C. Barley fonds, 5112
Art Director: Chris Byrd
Editor: Nora L. Deans
Project Coordinator: Lisa Oakley
National Park Service Coordinators: Karl Gurcke, Sandy Snell-Dobert, Cynthia Von Halle

Alaska Geographic is a nonprofit bookstore, publisher, educator, and supporter of Alaska's parks, forests, and refuges. Connecting people to Alaska's magnificent wildlands is at the core of our mission. A portion of every book sale directly supports educational and interpretive programs in Alaska's public lands. Learn more and become a supporting member at: **www.alaskageographic.org**

810 East Ninth Avenue
Anchorage, AK 99501
www.alaskageographic.org

ISBN-13: 978-0-930931-56-8

Library of Congress Catalog Card Number 2006103485

Printed in China

Dreams of Gold and Glory

KLONDIKE GOLD RUSH NATIONAL HISTORICAL PARK

CONTENTS

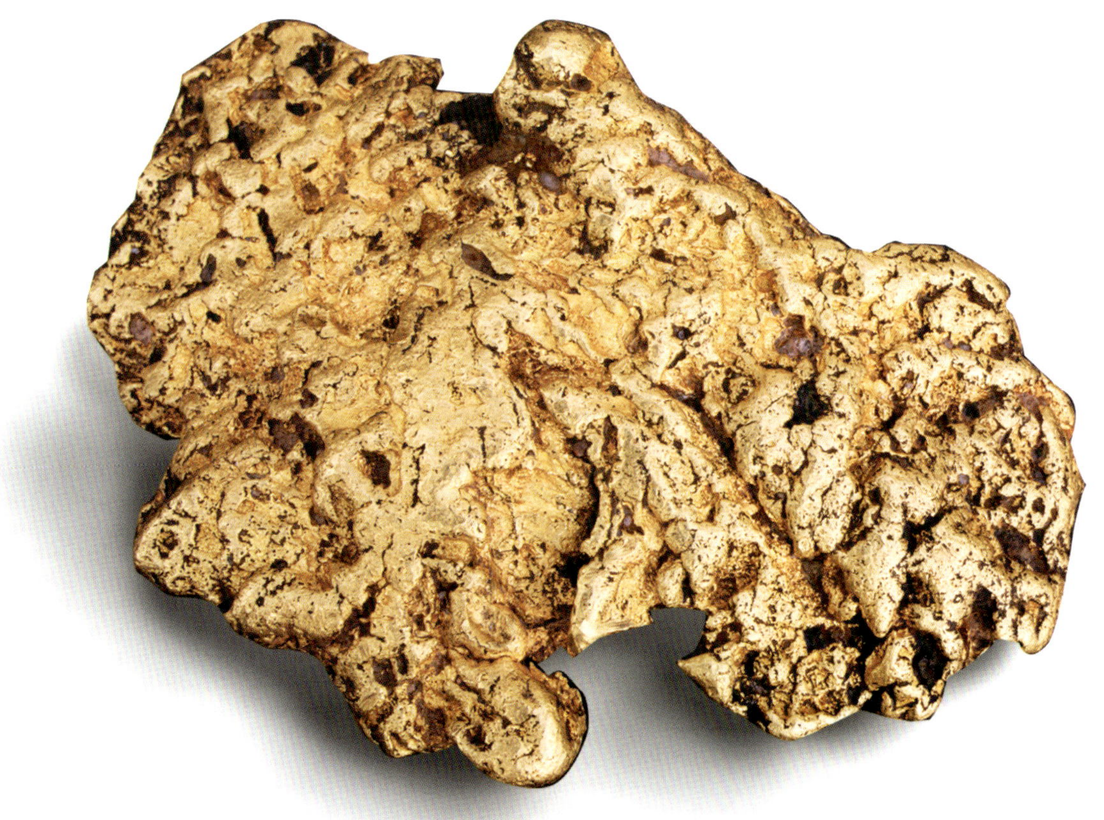

THE SEATTLE POS

SEATTLE, WASHINGTON, SATU

VOL. XXXII., NO. 62.

LATEST NEW

9

GOLD! GOLD! GOLD! G

Sixty-Eight Rich Me the Steamer Portla

STACKS OF YELLOW M

Some Have $5,000, Many Have a Few Bring Out $100,000

THE STEAMER CARRIES

Gold!

INTELLIGENCER.

EIGHT-PAGE EDITION.

JULY 17, 1897.

FROM THE KLONDIKE.

LOCK EDITION.

moment, so the tug was ordered sent to Seattle with the correspondent on board.

The Sea Lion, Capt. Sprague, made the trip down in record-breaking time, arriving at 6 o'clock, at least two hours ahead of the Portland.

The Portland has on board 68 miners with $700,000 in gold—not a man who has less than $5,000. Some of them have over $100,000. Some of them are Seattle men, and they come back happy and rich.

This story, obtained under considerable difficulty, but which is thought to be full and reliable in detail will be read with intense interest. It follows:

BRINGING BACK GOLD.

Sixty-eight Miners on the Portland Confirm the Fabulous Stories.

ON BOARD STEAMSHIP PORTLAND, 3 a. m.—At 3 o'clock this morning the steamship Portland, from St. Michaels for Seattle, passed up Sound with more than a ton of solid gold on board and 68 passengers. In the captain's cabin are three chests and a large safe filled with the precious nuggets. The metal is worth nearly $700,000 and the most of it was taken out of the ground in less than three months of last winter. In size the nuggets range from the size of a pea to a guinea egg. Of the 68 miners aboard hardly a man has less than $7,000 and one or two have more than $100,000 in yellow

inal discoverers of the El Dorado district.

Although most of the passengers are returning home with plenty of gold, they all advise and urge people who contemplate going to the Yukon not to think of taking in less than one ton of grub, and plenty of clothes. While it is a poor man's country, yet the hardships and privations to be encountered by inexperienced persons unused to frontier life is certain to result in much suffering during the winters. They should go prepared with at least a year's supplies.

The rush to the Klondike region commenced late last year and the claims were staked out and worked all winter. Labor was worth $15 a day last winter. Flour sold for $60 a sack and other provisions were proportionately high. Some of the mine owners attempted to lower the wages to $10 without success. By burning the ground to thaw the gravel, which was hoisted up about twelve feet to the dumps, where it was sluiced and washed in the spring, miners were able to work during the entire winter. In the early part of last month the thermometer ran up to 85 degrees in the shade and in January it was 58 degrees below zero.

The steamer Portland was reported passing Cape Flattery at 4:30 o'clock yesterday afternoon. The news dispatches from San Francisco announcing the arrival of the Excelsior at that port with many miners and a large quantity of gold has created a public demand for the latest and most authentic news from the gold fields of Alaska.

Realizing the impossibility of the Portland arriving in Seattle before 8 or 9

a man on board who has less than $5,000, and one or two have over $100,000."

The captain then went below and awakened one or two of his passengers, who came to the cabin and chatted a few moments about the Klondike and its mines.

Clarence Berry.

Clarence Berry is regarded as the luckiest man in the Klondike. With a miner it is all uck, nothing else. Ten months ago Mr. Berry was a poor miner and today he is in Seattle on his way to his home in Fresno, Cal., with $130,000 in gold nuggets. He said rather modestly:

"Yes, I've been rather fortunate. Last winter I took out $130,000 in 30 box lengths. A box length is 12x15 feet, and in one length I found $10,000. Another time, the second largest nugget ever found in the Yukon was taken out of my claim; it weighed 13 ounces and was worth $231.

"I have known men to take out $1,000 a day from a drift claim. Of course, the gold was found in pockets; and those finds, you can rest assured, were very scarce.

I would not advise a man to take in an outfit that would cost less than $500. He must exuect to be disappointed and the chances are that he may prospect for years without finding a paying claim, and again he may be lucky enough to strike it rich.

"The country is wild, rough and full of hardships for those unused to the rigors of Arctic winters. If a man makes a fortune he is liable to earn it by severe hardship and sufferings. But, then, grit, perseverence and luck will probably reward a hard worker with a comfortable income for life."

Inspector Strickland.

At 3 o'clock this morning the steamship Portland, from St. Michaels for Seattle, passed up Sound with more than a ton of solid gold on board and 68 passengers. In the captain's cabin are three chests and a large safe filled with the precious nuggets. The metal is worth nearly $700,000 and the most of it was taken out of the ground in less than three months of last winter. In size the nuggets range from the size of a pea to guinea egg. Of the 68 miners aboard hardly a man has less than $7,000 and one or two have more than $100,000 in yellow nuggets.

—*Seattle Post-Intelligencer*, July 17, 1897

Hardships and heartbreak. Dreams of gold and glory. The Klondike gold rush left a legacy of human failure and triumph. Its drama remains etched on the landscapes and communities it left behind, a story that lives on in Seattle and Skagway, Dawson City and the Yukon, and is preserved in a group of national parks straddling the border of two nations.

What kindled this outbreak of gold fever? Like lightning in a dry forest, word of the discovery of gold in the Yukon set people on fire with "Klondicitis," triggering a horde of "stampeders" who flocked north to Seattle, and beyond. Mayors and bankers, farmers and mill workers, men and women—people from all walks of life abandoned everything they owned, endured hardships, and spent their last dollar to get to an unknown land.

Why were thousands of ordinary people so quick to abandon their families and gamble away everything, including their lives, in a rugged landscape of mountains and ice so far away?

Gold! Gold! Gold! Gold!

America was a tinderbox of despair in mid-1897 when the headline that sparked this mass exodus was printed. Nearly half of all Americans, and many Europeans, lived at or below the poverty level. As a diversion from desperation, these Victorian-era citizens immersed themselves in tales of adventure and optimism—Jules Verne and H. G. Wells supplied otherworldly fantasies, while Horatio Alger preached his "bootstrap" philosophy.

The prospect of gold and escape from the ordinary lured many north to make their fortune, or die trying. Many did. Others had nothing to lose and everything to gain. A few were successful, but quickly lost their fortunes to gamblers or thieves or alcohol. Some settled in the new lands, making their fortune off others.

But these lands weren't empty when prospectors first ventured north. Interior First Nations people and coastal Chilkoot/Chilkat Tlingits tried—in vain—to control the human flood washing over them, but were ultimately overwhelmed and engulfed. Their cultures and lands were forever changed, the scars still evident in the remnants of trails reclaimed by the rainforest and the once-flourishing towns that now harbor only ghosts. The Tlingit language and rich cultural traditions were nearly lost as a result of the huge changes that began during the gold rush.

Though it was short in duration, the great Klondike gold rush of 1897–98 changed the course of history, and forever changed the lives of all it touched. More than a hundred years later, national park visitors feel some of the stampeders' excitement and challenge as they immerse themselves in the lives, loves, and losses of those hopeful prospectors who left their homes over a century ago.

Traversing a Rugged Landscape

Heavy snowfall made conditions difficult for Klondikers. Barely visible in the center of the picture is the roof top of the White Pass Hotel otherwise buried in snow.

It rises far away in the midst of the blue peaks of the Chilkoots, which grow bluer and bluer until they merge into the sky. The sides of the mountains slope at an angle of some forty-five degrees, and against their tops lie eternal glaciers and patches of snow.

—Tappan Adney, journalist, *The Klondike Stampede*, 1900

The stampeders of the Klondike gold rush faced many challenges in their journey north. Perhaps the most difficult was the spectacular yet rugged environment of Southeast Alaska. Fierce weather buffeted travelers facing steep mountains, while heavy snowpack increased their risk of being swept away by an avalanche in winter or drowning in white-water rapids full with snowmelt in spring. Dense forests and unfamiliar wildlife added to their travails.

It would have been a far different gold rush if there were no Coast Mountains, or if the deadly avalanche of April 3, 1898, had been triggered on the White Pass instead of the Chilkoot. If the head-waters of the Yukon River had not been where they are, perhaps Skagway and Dyea would never have developed.

Today, hiking in the northern coastal forest of Southeast Alaska, it's difficult to picture the chaos of the Klondike gold rush, or to feel the dynamic forces—glacial floods, tsunamis, avalanches, underwater landslides, erosion, earthquakes and rebounding land freed from the weight of massive glaciers—that continue to shape this astonishing land and coast.

Where glaciers once carved valleys from rock, wildlife now roams amid unmarred scenic beauty. At the very northern tip of the lush rainforests lining the Inside Passage lies Lynn Canal, undisturbed but for cruise ships, ferries, and recreational boaters.

Quieter still are two valleys at the far north end of Lynn Canal, which once hosted two of the most famous trails to the gold fields: the Chilkoot Trail of the Taiya River Valley and the White Pass Trail of the Skagway River Valley. The trails through these two valleys,

Glaciers form at high, cold altitudes where snow accumulates faster than it melts. As it accumulates, its weight increases, pressing out internal air and producing a river of ice that slides slowly downhill, carrying bits of earth and rock with it to the sea.

prized by Tlingit traders and later gold-rush stampeders, offered short pathways to glacier-free passes through otherwise impenetrable mountains. Bennett Lake lay beyond, linking travelers to the Yukon River watershed, Dawson City, and gold.

The formation of the Skagway and Taiya river valleys is a drama that continues to unfold. Millions of years ago, two of the plates that make up the Earth's crust, the Pacific Plate and the North American Plate, collided. The impact forced the Pacific Plate beneath the North American Plate, which buckled, folded, and was thrust upward, creating jagged coastal mountains. As the Pacific and North American plates continued their collision course, magma, or molten rock, oozed its way up through cracks in the plates, cooled slowly below the surface and became huge bodies of granite called plutons. Over the many millions of years it took to shape these valleys, weather and erosion carved away the land, exposing massive, eternally snow-capped granite mountains and deep, glacially carved valleys around Skagway and Dyea.

Some 50,000 years ago, 5,000-foot-thick glaciers filled the Skagway and Taiya river valleys up to the mountain peaks. Over 11,000 years ago, the ice began melting and the glaciers retreated, leaving narrow U-shaped valleys and massive rock "shoulders" bordering deep fjords, such as Lynn Canal and Taiya Inlet. Lynn Canal, a saltwater fjord, runs deep into the heart of the mountains.

As the massive glaciers retreated up-valley, the weight on the Earth's crust lessened, and the land began to rise, a process called isostatic rebound. Skagway itself has risen about 6 feet since a human flood of gold seekers washed through little more than a hundred years ago.

Stampeders passing through Skagway stayed relatively dry considering the region's climate. A rain shadow cast on the area by the Chilkat Range to the west shields Skagway from the worst of the storms. With an average of only 26 inches of precipitation each year, the Skagway and Taiya river valleys are so dry that they have a history of wildfires, which are extremely rare in the rest of Southeast Alaska. Neighboring areas are much wetter—Haines soaks up 50 inches of rain annually, while Juneau might get 90 inches, and soggy Ketchikan averages 200 inches.

The gold rush communities of Skagway (right) and Dyea (upper left) sit at the end of the ninety-mile-long Lynn Canal in deep glacier-carved valleys. Stampeders had to choose either the White Pass out of Skagway or the Chilkoot Trail out of Dyea; either way involved steep climbs over the Coastal Mountains.

LOOKING DOWN SKAGUAY RIVER FROM PORCUPINE HILL

A miner's work was never done. Here a miner cleans gold dust for shipment. Often black sand and heavy pebbles would be sluiced along with the gold. Magnets could be used to remove iron ore. Not as backbreaking as the rest of gold mining, but it still involved a lot of hand work.

Veins of Gold

Gold seekers reaching Skagway may have stayed relatively dry, but they found no gold there. The gold lay about 550 miles north, beyond the steep peaks of the coastal range. The only wealth to be discovered in Skagway and Dyea was in the pockets of stampeders on their way to the gold fields. There, in the vicinity of present-day Dawson, near the junction of the Klondike and Yukon rivers, rich veins of quartz held one of the largest concentrations of gold in the world, unused for millions of years before being noticed by prospectors in the late nineteenth century.

The veins of gold formed underground as a result of the movement of the Earth's plates. As magma rose under pressure, it forced its way into cracks in the overlying rock layers. Water circulating near the magma became hot enough to dissolve minerals from the surrounding rock. Then, as the water with its dissolved minerals rose through cracks and crevices, it gradually cooled, losing its ability to hold the minerals in solution. Gold, sulfur and other minerals deposited in these underground cracks solidified and hardened, lacing the rock in which they were concentrated with their glittering seams.

Millions of years of uplift and erosion eventually exposed the gold to the elements, and nuggets and flakes washed down the streams and creeks of the Klondike River drainages. Because gold is much heavier than sand and dirt, it sinks to the bottom of the streams, where it lies winking in the sunshine until plucked from icy waters by human hands.

One hundred thousand persons, it is estimated, actually set out on the Klondike Trails; some thirty or forty thousand reached Dawson... a few hundred found gold in quantities large enough to call themselves rich. And out of these fortunate men, only the merest handful managed to keep their wealth.

—Pierre Burton, *Klondike Fever*

Tapestry of Forest and Alpine Tundra

Prospectors, stampeders, or "Klondikers" as they would come to be known, encountered many different ecosystems along their hard trek north, but few if any knew they were trudging through a biological hot spot. In the Skagway and Taiya river valleys, coastal forest,

Routes to Gold

Before pocketing any amounts of gold, prospectors first had to get to the gold fields. Several routes led north. First, the "All-Canadian" route, beginning in Edmonton, Alberta, was advertised as a wagon road over the prairie. It was actually a 1,500-mile-long trek through unimproved wilderness; few succeeded in reaching the gold fields via this route.

The "Ashcroft Trail," beginning in Ashcroft, British Columbia, traversed the Canadian Rockies at elevations that were almost always covered by snow—another basically impassable route, although a number of stampeders tried it.

The "All-American" route, starting in Valdez, Alaska, was the shortest way to the Klondike, but was a lie from start to finish, since the gold fields were in Canada, and the route led directly over miles and miles of uncharted glaciers. Many gold-seekers died of exposure or starvation, or froze to death trying to navigate the steep, slippery, and crevassed glaciers found along this route.

The "All-Water" route involved travel by ocean-going steamship to western Alaska and then a 2,200-mile-long journey up the Yukon River by riverboat. It was the easiest, but certainly the most expensive, trip, earning the name "Rich Man's" route. It also had its share of danger. Shipwrecks were common on the rough passage across the Gulf of Alaska. Riverboats occasionally found themselves grounded on the shifting sands of the Yukon River; during "freeze up" at the beginning of winter, they were also sometimes caught hundreds of miles from Dawson, with nowhere to go.

The most highly touted, popular and accessible routes took stampeders from Seattle or other West Coast ports up the Inside Passage via steamship to Skagway or Dyea, then over either the Chilkoot or White Pass trails to Lake Bennett at the headwaters of the Yukon River. Prospectors then made their way down the Yukon in small boats to Dawson. Travelers most often chose the Skagway and Dyea trails for the same reason rivers and ice followed these paths: they represent the points of greatest geologic weakness. Faults that encouraged ice to carve deeper valleys also made an easier climb for people struggling from sea level to the summits.

Whichever route you chose, you will wish you had chosen the other.

—Tappan Adney, journalist

Trails to the Klondike Gold Fields 1897-98

Edmonton "Backdoor Routes"

All American "Glacier Routes"

Ashcroft Route

All Water Route "Richman's Route"

Chilkoot and White Pass Routes

interior forest and alpine tundra converge, and plants and animals from one mingle with those of the others. In one of many surprising examples, arctic ground squirrels and pika from the Interior thrive in the upper reaches of coastal river valleys. Some botanists say the area around the head of Lynn Canal, near Skagway, represents the greatest center of plant diversity in Alaska.

Coastal forests and beaches line the shores of the Inside Passage. Had more of the stampeders passed through the region in summer, they would have hiked through a dense concentration of plants flourishing in the long summer days, bathed by plentiful moisture. Lush greenery, including hemlock, spruce, birch, alder and devil's club, thrived in this climate, as they do today. But most gold-seekers saw nary a green leaf when they passed through here on their grim winter trek.

Once beyond the forest, stampeders came to know the deep snow, wind, and biting cold of winter in the starkly beautiful alpine habitat, which begins at roughly 2,500 feet above sea level. Barren by comparison with the rainforest, the meadows and hills in this zone fairly burst to life every summer with wildflowers, insects, and birds.

After successfully navigating through the forest and over alpine passes, the stampeders then faced the challenge of the Interior's boreal forest, with its greater extremes in weather—brutal heat in summer and extreme cold in winter. The forest was home for moose, caribou, bears, and other mammals, and prime breeding ground for the travelers' nemesis: the mosquito!

Most stampeders missed seeing the beautiful fall colors of the higher elevations. The majority arrived after the colors faded and snow covered the landscape. It was easier to ascend the steep passes with deep snowfields covering the rocky terrain of the passes.

Sampling of Species

Blueberry	*Vaccinium* spp.
Highbush cranberry	*Viburnum edule*
Sitka mountain ash	*Sorbus sitchensis*
Devil's club	*Oplopanax horridus*
Red-osier dogwood	*Cornus stolonifera*
Sub-alpine fir	*Abies lasiocarpa*
Sitka spruce	*Picea sitchensis*
Shore pine	*Pinus contorta contorta*
Black cottonwood	*Populus trichocarpa*
Paper birch	*Betula papyifera*
Dolly Varden char	*Salvelinus malma*
Coho/"Silver" salmon	*Oncorhynchus kisutch*
Hooligan	*Thaleichtys pacificus*
Bald eagle	*Haliaeetus leucocephalus*
Common raven	*Corvus corax*
Northwestern crow	*Corvus caurinus*
Mew gull	*Larus canus*
Steller's jay	*Cyanocitta stelleri*
Swainson's thrush	*Catharus ustulatus*
Pine siskin	*Carduelis pinus*
Golden-crowned kinglet	*Regulus satrapa*
Varied thrush	*Lxoreus naevius*
Black bear	*Ursus americanus*
Brown bear	*Ursus arctos*
Red squirrel	*Tamiascirus hudsonicus*
Beaver	*Castor canadensis*
Porcupine	*Erethizon dorsatum*
Mountain goat	*Oreamnos americanus*
Western toad	*Bufo boreas*

Bald eagles are a common sight in Southeast Alaska all year long.

Clockwise from top: red squirrel, Devil's club, and black bear.

RESTAU

Living in the Far North

Long before the discovery of gold and the Klondike stampede, the Chilkoot Tlingit people used the passes over the mountains as lucrative trade routes. They tried to maintain control of the ancient routes but were eventually over come by the shear numbers of gold-seekers flowing into their valleys.

When a man journeys into a far country, he must be prepared to forget many of the things he has learned, and to acquire such customs as are inherent with the existence in the new land...

—Jack London, *In a Far Country*

In the early 1800s, Euro-American explorers arrived in what is now Southeast Alaska, British Columbia and the Yukon Interior, and found they were not alone—these lands were already occupied by thriving groups of aboriginal people. What would later be the town of Dyea belonged to the enterprising Chilkoot and Chilkat Tlingit peoples. They had established five trade trails into the Interior, one of which was the Chilkoot Trail. The Raven clan of the Chilkoot tribe, the Lukaaxh.ádi, controlled the area now known as the Chilkoot Trail, which they referred to as A Shakee, "On Top of It." Other clans controlled the other trails.

This Chilkoot tribe traded with their northern neighbors, the Tagish First Nations people who lived in the area of Carcross and the along the Yukon and Klondike rivers. The Tlingit lived off the bounty of their land, trapping and hunting mammals and fishing for salmon, halibut, and eulachon. Berries and herbs were bountiful and were gathered for food and medicine, and strong trees provided excellent lumber for homes and canoes. The Tagish had better access to mammals and traded tanned moose and caribou hides and beaver, lynx, and fox pelts as well as copper with their southern neighbors.

Beginning in the early 1800s, Tlingits also successfully traded with Europeans and Americans, serving as intermediaries between the newcomers and some of the Interior Tlingit and First Nations peoples. When Europeans tried to trade directly with these groups by opening a post at Fort Selkirk in 1848, the Chilkoot Tlingit traveled over 500 miles to seek a solution and, in 1852 seized and destroyed the fort to maintain their trade dominance.

Trade Routes

The fur trade focused attention on the trade routes, but the Tlingits kept non-Natives from using the Chilkoot and Chilkat passes until 1880, when internal strife between the Chilkat and Chilkoot Tlingit broke out. Taking advantage of these internal conflicts, the U.S. military, led by Navy Commander Lester A. Beardslee and backed by a strategic display of the impressive new Gatling gun, asked the Tlingits to allow the non-Natives access to the Chilkoot Trail. That year also marked the beginning of the arrangement between white prospectors and Tlingit packers. This had a negative consequence, however. Contact with early prospectors and later, the gold rush stampeders, stressed both the Native cultures and the ecological balance of their homelands, and many Tlingits died as a result.

An increase in trade and small discoveries of gold in the Yukon caught the eye of the United States Army. On May 22, 1883, an army party began one of the first major expeditions over the Chilkoot Pass into Canada. Leading the party was Lieutenant Frederick Schwatka, who wanted to chart the lay of the land and find out if the Native inhabitants were a threat to America. Schwatka was shocked by what he thought were exorbitant packing fees charged by Tlingit packers—up to $13 per 100 pounds—but he changed his tune upon seeing the men and women make their way up the pass:

> *I ... in no way blamed the Indians for their stubbornness in maintaining what seemed at first to be exorbitant [fees], and only wondered that they would do this extremely fatiguing labor so reasonably.*

In spite of this glowing endorsement, the reluctance or downright refusal of newcomers to pay packers angered and befuddled the Tlingit, especially Lunáat', the Tlingit Raven Clan leader in charge of the Chilkoot. The infusion of newcomers overwhelmed the established Tlingit packing system and opened the door for opportunists eager to take their piece of the pie. One of those was trader John J. Healy, who, with business partner Edgar Wilson, opened the Healy & Wilson Trading Post sometime in 1884 at Dyea.

When Healy decided to "improve" the Chilkoot Trail for prospectors coming to the country in ever-greater numbers, Lunáat' took exception, and pleaded with the United States government:

> *I, Lunáat' chief of the Chilkoot tribe, make the following statement: Mr. Haley [Healy] wishes to take away our road or trail to the Yukon, which my tribe does not like, as we made it long ago, and it has always been in my tribe. We fixed the road good so that miners would not get hurt, and Mr. Haley is putting sticks or logs on it, so he can get pay for people going in over our trail, and we do not want to see that….*

What entrepreneurs did not understand was that Lunáat's plea came not only from commercial interest, but also from principle. According to Tlingit law, any injury or death occurring on the trail was the responsibility of the clan—therefore, Lunáat' wanted the risk to be incurred only by his experienced packers.

Although he was able to thwart Healy's toll road, competition from other Tlingits caused his downfall. Violence erupted when Tlingit packers from Sitka came to Dyea in June 1888 to take advantage of the booming packing business. Chief Jack of the Sitka Tlingits was killed in this battle, as was Lunáat', who died defending his clan's rights. Although Lunáat's duties fell to his sister, Raven Clan's management of the trail was never again as strong. Perhaps the greatest factor in the failure of the Tlingit trail management was not the infighting but the flood of stampeders during the gold rush, which overwhelmed the Tlingits in Dyea.

Border Country

Trail management was not the only dispute in the region. With the discovery of gold in the Forty-Mile watershed in 1886, not far from the future site of Dawson City, defining the always-fuzzy border between Canada and Alaska became more of an issue. Miners and traders knew it fell along the 141st Meridian, as negotiated in the Russian–British Treaty of 1825, but weren't sure of its exact location. Even after America bought out Russia's interest in these northern lands in 1867, the boundary dispute lay dormant until the discovery of gold.

To resolve the boundary issue, William Ogilvie was sent by Canada's minister of the interior in May 1887 to survey the 141st Meridian. Among his party was a 65-year-old grizzled war veteran, Captain William Moore. Moore had long enjoyed a robust pioneer life.

During his exploration of the Forty-Mile area in 1886, Moore's son Billy wrote to his father of a pass to the east of the Chilkoot, which was lower and supposedly easier than the Chilkoot. At Captain Moore's insistence, Ogilvie sent Moore and a Native guide, Keish ("Skookum Jim" Mason), to see for themselves. Skookum Jim was a Tagish/Tlingit guide known for his strength as a packer (hence the Chinook name "Skookum," which means "strong").

What they discovered was less a trail than a nightmare. "It was hard work getting through," Ben Moore would later write of his father's journey. "The mosquitoes were very bad, all the streams were swollen, there was dense underbrush, and traveling over and around rocky bluffs way above the canyons, but on nearing the summit and after reaching it, the going to Lake Bennett was much better."

Captain Moore and Skookum Jim caught up with the Ogilvie party at Lake Lindeman. Later, much to their amazement, Moore and his youngest son Ben, who was also traveling in the Interior, met up along the Pelly River. Captain Moore convinced his son that the lower

Captain William Moore

German-born William Moore set out to seek his fortune as a sea captain. Immigrating to America, he piloted tow-boats on the Mississippi, fought in the Mexican–American war, and sought gold in California and Canada. Moore and his three sons made their first fortune skippering steamboats on the Stikine River during the Cassiar gold rush in 1876, but lost it all when the gold died out.

Around 1884 John J. Healy and Edgar Wilson established a small trading post in the Dyea area. It is believed to be among the oldest in Southeast Alaska communities.

pass was an outstanding business opportunity, accurately predicting that the small trickle of miners going north would very soon multiply exponentially, and that the White Pass (so named by Ogilvie in honor of Sir Thomas White, Canadian Minister of the Interior) would be the better choice than the Chilkoot for a toll road and, eventually, a railroad.

Mooresville

Moore and his son left the Ogilvie party and traveled south, down the Chilkoot Trail to Dyea, where they took refuge at the Healy & Wilson Trading Post, gleaning additional information from John Healy. After a month in Juneau gathering supplies, the two made their way up Lynn Canal in canoes. Arriving at Skagway Bay on October 20, 1887, they wasted no time constructing a wharf for the commerce that Captain Moore knew would come, and a log cabin for themselves. As Ben later recalled, "I have never forgotten my father's words to me. 'Here,' said he, 'we will cast our future lots and try to hew out our fortune,' as I struck my axe into our first tree." ■

Skagway's (above) and neighboring Dyea's docks had to extend across mudflats and beyond low tide to reach waters deep enough for ships to safely dock.

What's Left of "Mooresville?"

Soon after arriving, Captain Moore and son Ben set about building what they called "Mooresville," and some of those buildings still stand today. The Moore Cabin, built during the fall of 1887 and the summer of 1888, is located near the corner of 5th Avenue and Spring Street. (It is not open to the public, although you can peek in the windows for a glimpse of the interior.) The cabin first served as proof for the Moore's homestead claim in the Skagway Valley, and later became a year-round residence when Ben and his family made the cabin their home in 1896.

In 1897, they started construction of the Moore House. Now a museum operated by the National Park Service, it was built in front of the cabin to hold Ben's growing family. In 1900, Ben moved the cabin 50 feet to the west to make way for additions to the house. Local businesswoman Hazel Kirmse bought the buildings in 1914, and her son, Jack Kirmse, sold them to the National Park Service in 1977. Extensive archaeological research and preservation work on both buildings reflect the park's skillful oversight.

Portland House, originally called the Moore Business Block, stands at the southeast corner of Fifth Avenue and State Street as a reminder of the commercial portion of Mooresville. The Business Block, built in 1897 by Captain Moore, was originally the location of the Moore Hotel, a commercial store space, a bank and law offices. The Skagway Chamber of Commerce, the Alaska Road Commission, and an army officer in charge of constructing Fort William Seward in Haines all later used the building for office space. It is now privately owned and undergoing meticulous and loving restoration by the owners, with technical assistance from the National Park Service.

Soldiers from the 106th Company, Coast Artillery line up in 1902 for Skagway's Fourth of July festivities in front of the Moore Hotel (Portland House), on the southeast corner of Fifth Avenue and State Street. This building still stands and the current owners have set out to rehabilitate the structure carefully adhering to the Secretary of the Interior's guidelines. The building is a contributing element in the Skagway Historic District and White Pass Historic Landmark.

Chasing Golden Dreams

Skookum Jim is credited with discovering the gold that started the Klondike gold rush.

Never will I forget it,
there on the mountain face,
Antlike, men with their burdens,
clinging in icy space;
Dogged, determined and dauntless,
cruel and callous and cold,
Cursing, blaspheming, reviling,
and ever that battle-cry—"Gold!"

—Robert Service, *The Trail of 'Ninety-Eight*

Like many gold rushes, the Klondike gold rush started with an accidental discovery. Skookum Jim, Captain Moore's Native guide on the previous White Pass reconnaissance, was sent on a mission by his mother to find one of his sisters, *Shaaw Tlaa* [Kate Carmack]. She had disappeared into the Yukon Territory shortly after marrying a white man named George Washington Carmack, and her mother wanted her to come home. Skookum Jim took his wife and his two nephews—*Kaa Goox* [Dawson Charlie] and *Koolseen* [Patsy Henderson]—with him. They later met up with George and Kate at the mouth of the Klondike River.

Once the two groups got together, they went fishing and hunting and were planning on logging to earn some money. They were also prospecting along what was then called Rabbit Creek, a tributary of the Thron [diuck] River (later called the "Klondike"). *Thron diuck* reportedly means "hammer water," so named by local Natives who pounded sticks into its shallow river bottom to support their salmon nets. Accounts of the actual discovery differ; George Carmack claimed to have found the gold, but Native oral tradition and William Ogilvie, who interviewed all the men, cite Skookum Jim as the finder. Arguments aside, once they traveled downriver and registered their claim in Forty-Mile, there is no disputing the fact that their discovery on August 16, 1896, launched one of history's more dramatic, well-publicized and bizarre migrations.

The Rush Begins

Word about the gold strike quickly spread within Alaska and the Yukon, setting off a rush from other mining towns such as Circle City and Forty-Mile. The newcomers mined over the winter, washed the tailing piles in the spring, traveled by river boat down the Yukon, and boarded the steamers *Excelsior* and *Portland* at St. Michael's, Alaska, as very rich men and women in the summer of 1897.

At 12 o'clock noon, amid the cheering of the vast crowd assembled on the dock, the Queen back out into the sound and soon we were well on our way to the North. We were now thinking seriously of the long trip and hard work yet to come.

—William Sharpe, stampeder

Only moments after the SS *Excelsior* docked in San Francisco on July 14, 1897, and the SS *Portland* offloaded passengers and payloads in Seattle three days later, newspapers were filled with that grand and glorious four-letter-word: GOLD! GOLD! GOLD! GOLD! It was said to be everywhere. You could pick it off the ground with your bare hands! Gophers could be trained to dig it up for you! People were getting rich overnight! A country suffering the effects of the Panic of 1893 (the economic depression of the 1890s) found the lure of easy money impossible to pass up. It seemed a dream come true.

Although cities like Vancouver, San Francisco and Portland tried to compete, Seattle soon became the "Gateway to the Klondike." The town's population nearly doubled between 1890 and 1900, thanks in large part to the arrival of the transcontinental railroad in 1893, an entrepreneurial spirit, connections to the northern trade routes, and, not least of all, the gold rush. One of those behind Seattle's success as the "official" supplier to the stampeders was Erastus Brainerd, a well-educated journalist who had moved there for health reasons.

Brainerd was appointed secretary of the Seattle Chamber of Commerce and devised a plan to tax the city's merchants and use the money to place exuberant advertisements in publications around the world. He also encouraged the Seattle Post-Intelligencer to publish a special Klondike edition on October 13, 1897. The issue's front page screamed "Seattle Opens the Gate to the Klondike Gold Fields!" It also featured a map of transcontinental railroad lines, illustrating that all railroads led to Seattle, "Gateway to the Klondike." The issue was shipped all over the country by train the next day.

Seattle's battle for the Klondike trade was so successful that it soon became the financial center of the Pacific Northwest. As people piled into the city, money poured out of their pockets and into the coffers of happy merchants. Concerned about the lack of supplies and provisions for the incoming hordes, the North West Mounted Police posted an order in February 1898 that required every miner entering Canada to bring with them enough provisions to last a year. Seattle merchants were only too happy to provide what usually turned out to be about 1,500 to 2,000 pounds of supplies per person. Some gold-seekers left more than $1,000 (in 1898 dollars; around $20,000 today) behind in Seattle when they departed for the gold fields.

What You Will Need

IN OUR LINE ON GOING TO THE ALASKA GOLD FIELDS.

ADOLPH A. DEKUM, HARDWARE, 111 FIRST ST., PORTLAND, OR.

Alaska Sled
Picks
Shovels
Axes
Hammer
Hatchet
Drawknife
Chisel
Planes
Square
Rule
Chalk Line
Axe Stone
Emery Stone
Pit Saw
Hand Saw
Files
Nails
Rope
Oakum
Pitch
Compass
Ice Creepers
Magnifying Glass
Magnets
Adjustable Tool Holder

YOU SAVE MONEY BY PURCHASING FROM US.

Gold Pan
Gold Scale
Axe Sheath
Knife Scabbard
Pack Strap
Sheet Steel Stove
Telescope Stove Pipe
Butcher Knife
Knives and Forks
Miner's Lamp
Lantern
Goggles
Cobbler's Repair Outfit
Calking Iron
Assortment of Bolts
Monkey Wrench
Common Table Ware
Granite Buckets
Aluminum Buckets
" Fry Pan
" Spoons
" Plates
" Coffee Pot
" Cups
" Bake Pan

TABLE OF DISTANCES.

ADOLPH A. DEKUM, HARDWARE, 111 FIRST ST., PORTLAND, OR.

Portland to St. Michaels	3186 Miles
St. Michaels to Dawson	1720 "
Portland to Skaguay	968 "
Skaguay to Lake Bennett	45 "
Portland to Dyea	974 "
Dyea to Summit Chilkoot Pass	15 "
Summit to head Lake Linderman	8 "
Head to foot Lake Linderman	4 "
Foot Lake Linderman to head Lake Bennett	5 "
Head to foot of Lake Bennett	22 "
Foot Lk. Bennett to Carribou Cross'g	3 "
Carribou Crossing to foot Tagish Lake	16 "
Tagish Lake to head Marsh Lake	5 "
Head to foot Marsh Lake	19 "
Foot Marsh Lake to head of Canyon	26 "
Head to foot of Canyon	1 "
Foot of Canyon to head of White Horse Rapids	1 "
Head to foot White Horse Rapids	2 "
Foot of Rapids to Tahkeena River	13 "
Tahkeena River to head Lk. La Barge	16 "
Head to foot Lake La Barge	30 "
Foot Lake La Barge to Big Salmon River	63 "
Big Salmon Riv. to Five Finger Rap.	95 "
Five Finger Rapids to Rink Rapids	6 "
Rink Rapids to Pelly River	53 "
Pelly River to White River	96 "
White River to Stewart River	10 "
Stewart River to Sixty Mile Post	20 "
Sixty Mile Post to Dawson City, at mouth of Klondike	49 "
Dawson City to Circle City	300 "

A Ton of Goods

Merchants, hoping to cash in on their own gold mine in sales, published booklets like this one above for prospectors to lure business their way. They included a mixture of information helpful to the eager stampeder. The Canadian Mounties required a year's supply of food, which along with equipment the miners needed added up to a ton or more. All of which needed, to be transported to the gold fields in the Yukon.

WASHINGTON TAILORING CO.
SOUTHERN HOTEL.
106
COOPER & LEVY.
104
COOPER & LEVY, PIONEER OUTFITTERS
SOUTHERN HOTEL ROOMS 25 50
COOPER & LEVY, PIONEER OUTFITTERS
PIONEER OUTFITTERS
COOPER & LEVY.
PIONEER OUTFITT
NORTHERN PACIFIC
TICKET OFFICE
SEATTLE THEATE
MONDAY TUESDAY JAN. 24-2
BLACK PATTI'S TROUBADOU

Seattle's Moran Brothers

One of the most enterprising businessmen to take advantage of the boom in Seattle was Robert Moran, two-term mayor of Seattle and president of his family's company, Moran Brothers' machine shop. The great Seattle fire of June 6, 1889 cost Seattle $10 million in loss of property, $40,000 of which was borne by Moran Brothers. They quickly rebuilt on 23 acres near the waterfront (the site of today's Seattle Seahawks football stadium); in their new shop, they could produce both wood and metal ships. Their timing was perfect; when news of the Klondike gold rush hit Seattle, the Morans were ready to meet the demand.

In January 1898, they started work on twelve riverboats and five barges set for delivery to St. Michael, Alaska. On May 24, Robert Moran led his impressive flotilla out of Elliott Bay and north on its treacherous voyage to the gold fields. It would not be an easy journey; what was supposed to take no more than thirty days actually took fifty-seven. Weather, especially near the Aleutian Islands, hampered the voyage. The sea claimed one riverboat and two barges along the way. Disappointing as this must have been for Robert Moran, it was actually quite remarkable, as it has been reported that 75 percent of the vessels crafted by other boat-builders up and down the West Coast for delivery to Alaska did not survive the trip, making Moran's journey one of the most successful in the story of the Klondike gold rush.

Up and Over the Passes

Of the estimated 100,000 souls who set out for the gold fields, most chose the Chilkoot or White Pass trails. They got to the trailhead towns of Skagway or Dyea via steamship, barge, or whatever "tub" was available. Then they were dumped—lock, stock, and heavy barrel—on the beaches at a rate of up to a thousand hopefuls a week. The quiet beauty of the Taiya and Skagway river valleys was shattered when the first boat arrived in Mooresville on July 29, 1897.

Tens of thousands of stampeders chose to land in Dyea and tackle the Chilkoot Trail, and an estimated 30,000 actually made it over the pass and into Canada. Perhaps 10,000 successfully climbed over White Pass, but far more turned back before they reached the passes. Some died or were killed, others were robbed by one of the region's notorious gangs, and then turned back because they had no operating funds. Entrepreneurial types set up businesses in the towns and along the trail, while others retreated after losing their outfits in some type of accident.

There was a rope stretched from Scales to summit, and I hugged that rope pretty closely all the way up that steep grade of 600 ft. All around us, as far the eye could reach, was snow and ice and the only foot holds were the holes stamped in the snow by this steady line of men climbing up the mountain.

—William Shape, stampeder, *Faith of Fools*

Early arrivals hired Tlingit packers, but the hordes of stampeders quickly overwhelmed the packers' capacity. As the trickle became a flood, thousands of people rushed in to form packing businesses to pick up the slack.

Most daunting about the Chilkoot route was the nightmarish final 800-foot climb to the summit of the pass. Because most stampeders were carrying 1,500 to 2,000 pounds of gear with them, many had to climb the entire 3,500-foot high hill twenty to forty times before all of their equipment was at the top and ready for inspection by North West Mounted Police. Over and over, a stampeder would carry 50 to 100 pounds on his back 5 miles or so up the trail to a new cache. Once at his new cache, he would drop his load and return for another. He went back and forth until his entire outfit was at the new cache. Then he'd repeat the exhausting process as he moved to another cache another 5 miles up the trail. The more people or animals he had, the more he could carry per trip and the faster it all went. Transportation was the key to success in getting to the gold fields. Some stampeders formed partnerships, working together to transport goods and protect them from theft or storm damage.

Early entrepreneurs carved out a rudimentary wagon road from Dyea to Canyon City and improved other portions of the trail. A wagon road was also built on the Canadian side, but it went only from lake to lake. No wagon road ran the entire length of the Chilkoot Trail.

To help ease the climb from Dyea to the summit, bridges sprang up over rushing streams, muddy sections of trail were "paved" with logs, and stairs were cut into the ice. But the greatest engineering feat on the Chilkoot was the completion of three aerial tramways during the dead of winter, 1897–1898.

The Dyea–Klondike Transportation Company, the smallest of the three, put the first aerial tramway into operation on the Chilkoot Trail and was one of the first tramways in the world powered by electricity. A gasoline-engine-powered aerial tramway, the second longest on the Chilkoot, was constructed by the Alaska Railroad and Transportation Company and was the next tramway to be put in operation.

The 9-mile-long Chilkoot Railroad and Transport Company was the longest of the three, and the most sophisticated. The company built two steam-engine-powered tramlines, one from Canyon City to Sheep Camp and the other from Sheep Camp to just north of the summit. At the Scales, the tramline spanned a distance of 2,200 feet between two towers, making it the world's longest span at the time.

Eventually, all three aerial tramways merged into a single entity, and charged seven-and-a-half cents per pound to haul goods from Dyea to Lake Bennett. In June 1899, the White Pass & Yukon Route railroad purchased the Chilkoot tramway companies and started dismantling them in January 1900 to eleminate competition.

Mooresville, or Skagway, as the U.S. Post Office soon renamed it, was still a viable choice for many. It offered a much better port than Dyea, especially after the completion of Moore's Wharf, and soon had four wharfs in operation. And although the White Pass Trail was longer than the Chilkoot Trail, the summit was 600 feet lower. On July 14, 1897, Captain Moore declared the White Pass Trail "open" and suitable for horses. But he did not anticipate the crush of naïve and inexperienced stampeders who brought horses and other livestock totally unsuitable for packing. Within two months traffic on the trail slowed to a crawl and then stopped altogether due to overuse and bad weather.

Before long, White Pass became known as "Dead Horse Trail," and anyone who dared it understood why. Legend recalls that as many as 3,000 horses died on the trail "like mosquitoes in the first frost," as Jack London, who joined the rush, would later write. "And from Skagway to Bennett they rotted in heaps.... Men shot them,

It looked to me, sir, like suicide. I believe a horse will commit suicide, and this is enough to make them; they don't mind the hills like they do these mud-holes. I don't know but that I'd rather commit suicide, too, than be driven by some of the men on this trail.

—Stampeder interviewed by journalist Tappan Adney

worked them to death, and when they were gone, went back to the beach and bought more.... Their hearts turned to stone, those that did not break, and they became beasts, the men on the Dead Horse Trail."

Among the eager entrepreneurs who flocked to both Skagway and Dyea during the Klondike gold rush was George A. Brackett, who, along with six of his seven sons, brought railroad and road-building expertise. He combined what was left of his own money with that of some modest investors; hired would-be miners frustrated with the agonizingly slow pace of the "rush"; and within a few months, built a respectable wagon toll road up the Skagway River Valley that was not only passable but lucrative.

After lugging their ton of goods up the Chilkoot Pass, many Klondike stampeders set up camp and built their boats on the shores of Lake Lindeman rather than carry their provisions all the way to Lake Bennett. To their surprise when the snow melted in the spring, it revealed churning rapids along the One Mile River between the lakes. Bigger and worse rapids lay ahead, but first they had to successfully navigate this short, but treacherous stretch.

Down River to the Gold Fields

It could take stampeders up to three months to cross the mountain passes and reach the Interior gold fields. Some of those who set out in the late summer and early fall of 1897 made it all the way to Dawson City before freeze-up, but once there, the specter of starvation caused some to turn and flee. Others arrived at the upper lakes too late by a day, a week or a month, and had to sit out the winter in tents hastily erected on the frozen shores.

Time became critical for stampeders like journalist Tappan Adney, who left Seattle in late summer, arrived in Skagway on August 20 and reached Dawson on October 31 amid icebergs. Freeze-up occurred shortly thereafter.

Many stampeders became disheartened in Lake Bennett, for they were still 550 miles from the actual gold fields. They busied themselves by building boats—many of which were nothing more than makeshift rafts—that they would use to float the rest of the way down the Yukon River when the ice broke. Finally, on May 29, 1898, the ice did break and the motley flotilla of 7,124 boats made its clumsy way toward the gold fields.

Unskilled and unprepared, many stampeders lost their boats—and some lost their lives—in the rapids near Whitehorse. Once the rapids were successfully navigated, those hardy souls who hadn't given up finally made their way on to Dawson, almost two years after gold was first discovered on Rabbit Creek. Unbeknownst to those seeing Dawson for the first time, and to those still on their

Gold mining is hard work. Miners devised elaborate systems for moving the gold-laden gravel to sluice boxes that would separate the gold from the worthless gravel. Some rich veins were buried under permafrost, so miners made fires to melt the ice and thaw the frozen ground to dig down to the "pay dirt."

way from Seattle to Skagway and Dyea, most of the good claims had already been secured by the prospectors who had rushed over from Circle City and Forty-Mile.

Stampeders coming to the gold fields in 1898 found that they had to search for gold in increasingly remote locations, or work for those who had already staked lucrative claims. Many became disheartened, selling their gear for pennies on the dollar and taking the next riverboat home. Those who stayed found mining a dirty, sweaty, backbreaking business. To get through the permafrost to where the gold was, miners built fires to melt shafts, digging as the earth thawed. Once they hit bedrock, they hoisted dirt, gravel, and gold-bearing "pay dirt" out of the hole and left them in piles, where they would be separated or sluiced by hand when water became available in the spring.

Boomtowns

The village of tents that was Mooresville quickly turned into a buzzing town of around 10,000 in just a few months, and what people thought of the town depended on who was asked. While one observer described it as "little better than hell on earth," others extolled its virtues. A town map officially adopted by the Skagway City Council on March 8, 1898, boasted:

> *SKAGUAY—The youngest city in the world has now a permanent population of no less than 4,000 people. Founded only last August it has steadily forged to the front … until today the Young City bears the proud distinction of being the Metropolis of Alaska, and the most prosperous town on the North Pacific Coast [sic] it already has a Church, a School, an Electric light system and water system.*

YUKON OUTFITTERS
MERCANTILE MINING

Today, little visual evidence remains of the former bustling town of Dye.

Dyea was advertised as a more respectable place to do business, but in reality, it was almost as rough as Skagway. By April 1898, Healy's hamlet had grown from one general store and a small Tlingit village into a town of about 8,000 semi-transient citizens.Competition for business between the towns of Skagway and Dyea was fierce—vitriolic editorial barbs flew back and forth between the rival newspapers almost weekly.

New villages along the trails ranged in reputation from somewhat dubious to downright nefarious. White Pass City, about 15 miles from Skagway on the White Pass Trail, lined the Skagway and White Pass river valleys with tents and the occasional wooden shack, which barely passed for accommodations. As gold-rush journalist Stroller White wrote:

> *[A]bout four miles south of the Summit there flourished for six months during the year of 1898 what was probably the toughest, most Godless town ever known in the North or anywhere else. It was called White Pass City and its name was the only decent thing about it. Its residents were mostly those who were considered, even then, too tough to live in Skagway.... White Pass City consisted mostly of tents but it also had sixteen buildings constructed of lumber and muslin.... There were seventeen saloons—one for each building and one at large...*

Sheep Camp, a more or less permanent settlement along the Chilkoot Trail, didn't fare much better, according to Tappan Adney:

> *The population of Sheep Camp may be classified as follows: those who have packed their own stuff thus far and are wavering, discouraged by bad weather; those moving their goods right through with horses or on their backs; professional gamblers; and a great swarm of men packing over the summit. These last are mostly hangers-on from Juneau, several being deserters from the*

April 17, 1898 [Summit of the White Pass]: Had a hard morning's work, opening boxes and bags, etc., to exhibit my things to the Customs Officers. They make you open up practically everything for inspection. Horrible job it is to do in a blizzard on the top of this mountain. Things get all covered with snow as fast as they are unpacked, and then have to be packed ready for sledding down the mountain. But at last it was done, and the outrageous duty they assessed me paid (60%), and I stepped across the boundary line into the territory of the Canadians as quickly as I could get ready to leave that dreary place.

—Frederick Stephen Wombwell, stampeder

The avalanche had tumbled from a peak twenty-five hundred feet above the trail, just about the Stone House. It covered ten acres to a depth of thirty feet. Within twenty minutes a thousand men from Sheep Camp were on the spot digging parallel trenches in an effort to locate the victims. The scene was a weird and terrible one... More than sixty perished. A handful were rescued alive, some of whom had been three hours under the snow.

—Pierre Breton, Klondike Fever

revenue-cutters, while others are men who were bound for Dawson, and who had the wit or presence of mind, which few others seemed to show, to recognize a gold-mine when it came before their eyes, even if not a Klondike one. They are making great money....

Settlements along the Chilkoot Trail fought off competition from Skagway and the White Pass Trail until a massive avalanche killed more than seventy stampeders near the Scales in April 1898. Stampeder traffic slowed considerably but still continued until construction of the White Pass & Yukon Route railroad from Skagway to Bennett wiped out packing on the Chilkoot and White Pass trails. Dyea and other Chilkoot Trail towns dried up, and White Pass City became a ghost town overnight. Even the thriving metropolis of Bennett, with its several thousand residents, quickly vanished when the train skirted Lake Bennett for Carcross and Whitehorse. Dawson, the town at the heart of the flurry, became a permanent home to many of those first entrepreneurs and their families. Fate was fickle, however, and most gold rush settlements came to a quick end. ■

Sheep Camp served as a natural halting-point along the Chilkoot Trail. Situated on the edge of the tree line it was the last place to collect timber or firewood. After this point it was all rock or snow for the remaining four miles leading to the top of the pass.

Soapy and Frank,

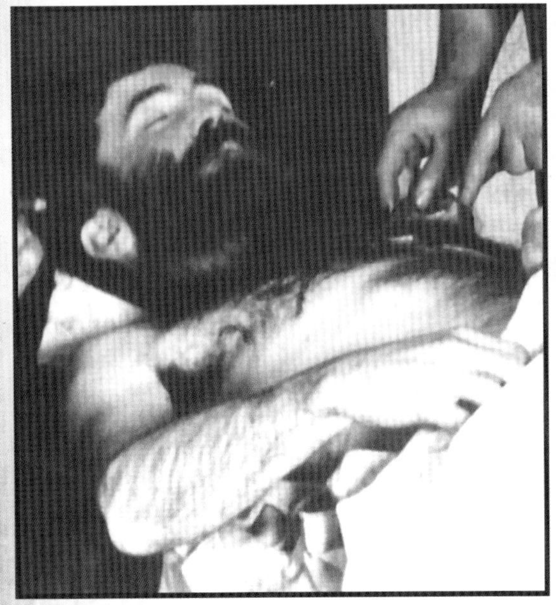

and Skagway's Gold Rush Cemetery

Jefferson Randolph "Soapy" Smith was a professional confidence man who came to Skagway in pursuit of fresh business after being kicked out of several lucrative cities in Colorado. Tired, disoriented, and loaded with cash, Skagway stampeders were easy pickings. Soapy and his gang of robbers and murderers were happy to relieve prospectors of their burden through trickery and deceit. Soapy also befriended Skagway's widows, orphans, and stray dogs. Frank Reid was a self-proclaimed virtuous town leader and the town surveyor, but he was no choir-boy either—he reportedly came to Skagway after killing a man in Oregon.

Clearly, Skagway wasn't big enough for both of them. A group called the "Committee of 101" elected themselves the "saviors" of Skagway and declared their mission of ridding their good city of its nefarious citizen. Soapy convened his own "Committee of Law and Order" but soon found himself in a gunfight with Frank. Soapy and Frank shot each other on Skagway's Juneau Wharf on July 8, 1898. Soapy died instantly, but Frank lingered for twelve days before dying of a bullet wound to the groin.

Both men were buried in the Gold Rush Cemetery north of Skagway. Frank's tomb, which claims "He Gave His Life For the Honor of Skagway," seems to have fewer visitors than Soapy's more modest grave, which lies outside the cemetery boundary.

Bower
ith's Saloon.
laska.
Jeff Smith.
Flash light
11 P.M.

PALACE MEAT MARKET
JANUARY
TREASURY DEPARTMENT
12
Remington

Preserving the Past

Today's stampede comes from visitors eager to re-live the gold rush. Klondike Gold Rush National Historical Park's visitor center is just one of a dozen buildings from the gold rush era in use today. Many belong to the National Park Service, but are leased to businesses that recreate the enterprises of the past.

The Klondike fever lasted just two years... But in that brief period, thousands of men lived a lifetime. In many ways the great quest was an approximation of life itself... Those who survived the experience and learned from it were made wise... At last they realized that the Klondike experience was as much a quest for self as it was for gold.

—Pierre Breton, *The Klondike Quest*

The Klondike gold rush was over in a flurry, much as it had begun. But when it died, it left the landscape and the lives of those caught in its hysteria greatly changed. Seattle had become a stronger, larger city and established itself as the financial and transportation hub of the Pacific Northwest. Although Dyea shuttered its windows and closed its doors, Skagway lived on, first as a railroad town, then as the bustling international tourist destination it is today. Whitehorse and Dawson, also popular with tourists, prospered as mining, government, and supply centers.

In 1933, president of the National Bank of Alaska and Skagway resident Elmer Rasmuson raised the idea of creating a "Chilcoot National Park" honoring the Klondike gold rush, but the idea didn't gather real steam until the 1960s. On June 30, 1976, President Gerald R. Ford authorized Klondike Gold Rush National Historical Park, creating four units in the United States—three in Alaska and one in Seattle—by signing Public Law 94-323.

Parks Canada established a historic site in Dawson City, Yukon Territory in 1972, and, more than twenty years later, in 1993, the Chilkoot National Historic Site came into existence.

In Skagway, many buildings had been vacant for years and all had taken a beating from the harsh Alaska climate by the time the park was established.

Archaeologists, historians, and historical architects were first on the scene, identifying important structures. They were followed by carpenters, electricians, plumbers and other skilled craftspeople. Ultimately, eighteen buildings in Skagway were acquired and rehabilitated or restored. Many gold rush-era buildings, while still owned and managed by the park, are leased by private businesses that cater to Skagway's booming tourism industry, generating employment opportunities and sales tax revenue for the community. The buildings also generate rental income for the park, which pays for their continuing

Leave Artifacts Where They Lay

Shortly before the Klondike Gold Rush National Historical Park was established, a popular recreation magazine announced to the world that the Chilkoot Trail was a "bottle collector's paradise." Many valuable artifacts left behind during one of the world's most exciting historical events found themselves in the backpacks and pockets of visitors. Most became part of private collections, where they rarely see the light of day, while others were later thrown in the garbage by family members who had no interest in or knowledge of these rusty relics of the past. Today, visitors must help preserve the park's character by leaving the remaining artifacts where they lay, so they can continue to tell their stories to all.

73
73

White Pass & Yukon Route

Railroad's Broadway Depot

Today, the White Pass & Yukon Route Railroad's Broadway Depot, built in 1898, and the adjacent railroad General Office Building, built in 1900, tell the story of early Skagway—but they were almost lost forever. By the 1960s, the buildings were too run-down for the railroad, which decided to demolish them. The WP&YR offered both the Depot and General Office buildings to the National Park Service, but in 1968, the national historical park was still in the early planning stages and no money could be allocated to purchase or restore the historic buildings.

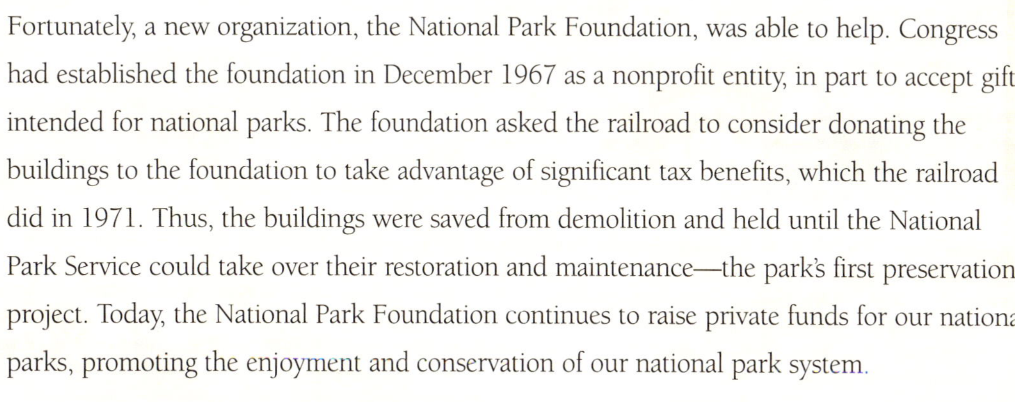

National Park Service officials lobbied for the preservation of the buildings, but had no actual power to stop demolition. Fortunately, a new organization, the National Park Foundation, was able to help. Congress had established the foundation in December 1967 as a nonprofit entity, in part to accept gifts intended for national parks. The foundation asked the railroad to consider donating the buildings to the foundation to take advantage of significant tax benefits, which the railroad did in 1971. Thus, the buildings were saved from demolition and held until the National Park Service could take over their restoration and maintenance—the park's first preservation project. Today, the National Park Foundation continues to raise private funds for our national parks, promoting the enjoyment and conservation of our national park system.

maintenance. The other historic buildings are used for visitor assistance, exhibits, museums, office space and employee housing.

The Seattle Unit of Klondike Gold Rush National Historical Park was created during the high point of the restoration of Pioneer Square. Thanks to preservation work with its partner, Historic Seattle, its visitor center in now in the Cadillac Hotel, one of the oldest buildings in Pioneer Square.

Following the Stampeder's Footsteps

Today, you can recreate your own gold rush odyssey through a system of parks in both the United States and Canada—known as the Klondike Gold Rush International Historical Park, established in 1998 through coordinated proclamations by United States President Bill Clinton and Canadian Prime Minister Jean Chrétien. This cooperative effort links a number of parks established to commemorate the gold rush: the Seattle, Skagway, White Pass, and Chilkoot Trail units of the Klondike Gold Rush National Historical Park in the United States, and the Chilkoot Trail National Historic Site, Thirty-Mile Section of Yukon River and Dawson Historical Complex National Historic Site in Canada.

Step back in time and imagine the chaos of frenzied stampeders buying supplies for the harsh journey ahead when you enter the Seattle Unit of Klondike Gold Rush National Historical Park in Seattle's Pioneer Square Historic District. Or "recreate" the stampeders' journey by boarding a cruise ship from Seattle or taking a ferry from Bellingham through the Inside Passage.

The gold rush comes to life upon arrival at the park's Visitor Center in Skagway, where walking tours, interpretive exhibits, and special programs make you feel as though you were one of the stampeders. Then, just as they faced over a hundred years ago, it's decision time. Hike up the Chilkoot Trail? Or take the easy route over the White Pass on the White Pass & Yukon Route Railroad?

Pullen and Pullen House Bus in Early Days

Tourism

The vast majority of stampeders found nothing but trouble in the Klondike, and most hightailed it out of the country as fast as possible. One who chose to stay—Harriet Pullen—became an early tourism promoter, and what a character she was.

Harriet Pullen came to Skagway at the height of its gold-rush excitement. She arrived penniless, claimed to be a widow (although her husband later showed up looking for her), and cooked and cleaned to support her children. She soon bought a string of packhorses for use on the dreaded Dead Horse Trail and claimed never to have lost a horse. Later, she leased and then bought Captain Moore's mansion and started a boarding house. This evolved into the legendary Pullen House Hotel, complete with a gold-rush museum, fresh produce and dairy products from her Dyea farm, and her creative fireside stories of gold rush characters and events.

Preserving the Past

Klondike Gold Rush National Historical Park is one of the few parks with boundaries that define the business district of a viable, active community. Park plans called for acquisition, restoration and use with an emphasis on keeping the historic district alive – with local citizens actively involved in its preservation.

Inside park boundaries lies the Skagway Historic District with more than one-hundred buildings, 19 of which are owned by the park. Here, both private and public interests join together to maintain a distinctive appearance of the gold rush era. Many buildings were relocated to Broadway around 1908 to create a "main street." The Historic District retains this look today giving visitors a visual sense of the real people and real events of the gold rush.

A key group of historic buildings owned and preserved by the park is the Mascot Saloon Group. The Mascot Saloon is now a museum including exhibits describing the saloon and early social life in Skagway. As one of the oldest and longest-lived saloons in boom town Skagway, the Mascot was restored by the park to its gold rush era appearance

Expanding the Historic District

Pictures, diaries and other objects from families of stampeders are often donated to the park for preservation. In 2008 the George and Edna Rapuzzi collection was donated to the park by the Rasmuson Foundation. This donation of the largest intact gold rush collection of original objects and buildings includes the saloon and headquarters of Jefferson Randolph "Soapy" Smith--Skagway's most infamous con-man during the Klondike gold rush. Donations like these strengthen the park's commitment to maintaining a cooperative spirit with the city of Skagway. Both city and park shared in the benefits of the Rasmuson generous donation.

The preservation of historical buildings in Skagway celebrates one of the most spectacular events of the late 19th century--the Klondike gold rush. The unique partnership of Klondike Gold Rush National Historical Park and the city of Skagway promotes responsible practices to preserve an irreplaceable cultural heritage.

The Mascot Saloon prior to the renovations made by the Klondike Gold Rush National Historical Park.

RED ONION
SALOON
RED ONION
1898
SALOON
GOLD RUSH
BROTHEL
PIZZA
THE TRAIL BENCH
SKAGWAY
GIFTS
Visitor Information
Center

Thousands of adventurous hikers choose to traverse the Chilkoot Trail every summer—this world-class backpacking route challenges even the most fit hiker. Both the trail and the easier train ride take you to Canada, where Parks Canada celebrates the Klondike gold rush with four national historic sites. Hikers on the Chilkoot Trail may top the summit and meet a Parks Canada warden at the warming hut. The adventure continues at the Thirty-Mile Section of the Yukon River, where swift waters and shifting sands challenged the skills of every sternwheeler pilot who tested it. Just like those stampeders stubborn enough to reach Dawson, you can walk down the streets of the Dawson Historical Complex National Historic Site, where preservation of gold rush-era buildings and interpretive exhibits recreate the hustle and bustle of years gone by. And finally, you can drive up Bonanza Creek to the Discovery Claim National Historic Site to see where it all began.

Successful Stampeders

John Nordstrom used his gold rush riches to establish a shoe store that later grew into the current upscale department store.

Clarence Berry made his first fortune in the Klondike, a second fortune in Fairbanks and a third in California oil.

C.C. Filson staked his claim in 1897 by outfitting stampeders from his store in Seattle with clothing and gear designed for the frigid north.

Sid Grauman failed at prospecting in the Klondike, but later succeeded in Hollywood creating one of Southern California's most recognizable and visited landmarks, Grauman's Chinese Theater.

There's gold, and it's haunting and haunting,
It's luring me on as of old;
Yet it isn't the gold that I'm wanting
So much as just finding the gold.
It's the great, big, broad land 'way up yonder,
It's the forests where silence has lease,
It's the beauty that thrills me with wonder,
It's the stillness that fills me with peace.
—Robert Service, The Spell of the Yukon